'I can promise to be candid, not, however, to be impartial.'

JOHANN WOLFGANG VON GOETHE
Born 1749, Frankfurt, Germany
Died 1832, Weimar, Germany

This selection is taken from *Maxims and Reflections*,
translated by Elisabeth Stopp,
Penguin Classics, 1998.

GOETHE IN PENGUIN CLASSICS
Faust, Part I
Faust, Part II
Maxims and Reflections
Elective Affinities
The Sorrows of Young Werther
Selected Poetry
Italian Journey 1786–1788

JOHANN WOLFGANG VON GOETHE

*Sketchy, Doubtful,
Incomplete Jottings*

Translated by
Elisabeth Stopp

PENGUIN BOOKS

PENGUIN CLASSICS

UK | USA | Canada | Ireland | Australia
India | New Zealand | South Africa

Penguin Books is part of the Penguin Random House group of companies
whose addresses can be found at global.penguinrandomhouse.com.

Penguin
Random House
UK

This selection published in Penguin Classics 2015
007

Translation copyright © the Estate of Elisabeth Stopp, 1998

Set in 10/14.5 pt Baskerville 10 Pro
Typeset by Jouve (UK), Milton Keynes
Printed in Great Britain by Clays Ltd, St Ives plc

A CIP catalogue record for this book is available from the British Library

ISBN: 978–0–141–39713–9

www.greenpenguin.co.uk

It is much easier to recognize error than to find truth; the former lies on the surface, this is quite manageable; the latter resides in depth, and this quest is not everyone's business.

*

We all live on the past and perish by the past.

*

When we are called to learn something great, we at once take refuge in our native poverty and yet have still learnt something.

*

The Germans are indifferent about staying together, yet they do want to be on their own. Each person, never mind who he may be, has his own way of being alone and is unwilling to be deprived of this.

*

The empirical-moral world consists largely of bad will and envy.

*

Superstition is the poetry of life; so it does the poet no harm to be superstitious.

*

Trust is a curious matter. Listen only to one person: he may be wrong or deceiving himself; listen to many: they are in the same case, and as a rule you don't really discover the truth.

*

One should not wish anyone disagreeable conditions of life; but for him who is involved in them by chance, they are touchstones of character and of the most decisive value to man.

*

A limited, honest man often sees right through the knavery of the sharpest tricksters.

*

One who feels no love must learn to flatter, otherwise he won't make out.

*

You can neither protect nor defend yourself against criticism; you have to act in defiance of it and this is gradually accepted.

*

The crowd cannot do without efficient people and always finds efficiency burdensome.

*

Anyone who tells on my faults is my master, even if it happens to be my servant.

*

Memoirs from above downwards, or from below upwards: they are always bound to meet.

*

If you demand duties from people and will not concede them rights, you have to pay them well.

*

When a landscape is described as romantic, this means that there is a tranquil sense of the sublime in the form of the past, or, what amounts to the same, of solitude, remoteness, seclusion.

*

The splendid liturgical song '*Veni Creator Spiritus*' is in actual fact a call addressed to genius; and this is also why it appeals powerfully to people who are spirited and strong.

*

Beauty is a manifestation of secret natural laws which without this appearance would have remained eternally hidden from us.

*

I can promise to be candid, not, however, to be impartial.

*

Ingratitude is always a kind of weakness. I have never known competent people to be ungrateful.

*

5

We are all so blinkered that we always imagine we are right; and so we can imagine an extraordinary spirit, a person who not only makes a mistake but even enjoys being wrong.

*

Completely moderate action to achieve what is good and right is very rare; what we usually see is pedantry seeking to retard, impertinence seeking to precipitate.

*

Word and image are correlatives which are always in quest of one another as metaphors and comparisons show us clearly enough. Thus, from of old, what is inwardly said or sung for the ear is at the same time intended for the eye. And so in ages which seem to us childlike, we see in codes of law and salvational doctrine, in bible and in primer, a continual balance of word and image. If they put into words what did not go into images, or formed an image of what could not be put into words, that was quite proper; but people often went wrong about this and used the spoken word instead of the pictorial image, which was the origin of those doubly wicked symbolically mystical monsters.

*

Anyone who devotes himself to the sciences suffers, firstly through retardations and then through preoccupations. To begin with, people are reluctant to admit the value of what we are providing; later on they act as though they already knew what we might be able to provide.

*

A collection of anecdotes and maxims is the greatest treasure for a man of the world – as long as he knows how to weave the former into apposite points of the course of conversation, and to recall the latter on fitting occasions.

*

People say, 'Artist, study nature!' But it is no small matter to develop what is noble out of what is common, beauty out of what lacks form.

*

Where concern is lost, memory fares likewise.

*

The world is a bell that is cracked: it clatters, but does not ring out clearly.

*

One must put up kindly with the pressing overtures of young dilettantes: with age they become the truest votaries of art and of the master.

*

When people really deteriorate, their only contribution is malicious joy in the misfortune of others.

*

Intelligent people are always the best encyclopaedia.

*

There are people who never make mistakes because they never have sensible projects.

*

Knowing my attitude to myself and to the world outside me is what I call truth. And so everyone can have his own truth and yet it remains the self-same truth.

*

What is particular is eternally defeated by what is general; the general has eternally to fit in with the particular.

*

No one can control what is really creative, and everybody just has to let it go its own way.

*

Anyone to whom nature begins to unveil its open mystery feels an irresistible yearning for nature's noblest interpreter, for art.

*

Time is itself an element.

*

Man never understands how anthropomorphic he is.

*

A difference which gives reason nothing to register is not a difference.

*

In phanerogamy there is still so much of what is cryptogamic that centuries will not suffice to unriddle it.

*

Exchanging one consonant for another might perhaps be due to some organ deficiency, transforming a vowel into a diphthong the result of conceited pathos.

*

If one had to study all laws, one would have no time at all to transgress them.

*

One can't live for everyone, more especially not for those with whom one wouldn't care to live.

*

A call to posterity originates in the clear vital feeling that there is such a thing as permanence and that even if this is not immediately acknowledged it will, in the end, win the recognition of a minority and finally of a majority.

*

Mysteries do not as yet amount to miracles.

*

I convertiti stanno freschi appresso di me. [The converted are puzzled by me.]

*

Reckless, passionate favouritism of problematic men of talent was a failing of my younger years of which I could never completely rid myself.

*

I would like to be honest with you without us parting company; but this isn't possible. You are acting wrongly and trying to sit between two stools, not getting any followers and losing your friends. What's to come of this!

*

No matter whether you're of high rank or low, you can't avoid paying the price of your common humanity.

*

Writers of a liberal persuasion are now on to a good game; they have the whole public at their feet.

*

When I hear talk about liberal ideas, I'm always amazed how people like to delude themselves with the sound of empty words: an idea is not allowed to be liberal! Let it be forceful, doughty, self-enclosed, so as to fulfil its God-given mission of being productive. Still less is a concept allowed to be liberal; for its commission is completely different.

*

But where we have to look for liberality is in people's attitudes and these are their feelings come to life.

*

Attitudes, however, are seldom liberal because an attitude springs directly from the person, his immediate context and his needs.

*

We'll leave it at that; by this yardstick we should measure what we hear day after day!

*

It's always only our eyes, the way we imagine things; nature quite alone knows what it wills, what it intended.

'Give me where I stand!'
Archimedes.

'Take where you stand!'
      Nose.
Declare where you stand!
      G.

It is general causal relationships which the observer will explore, and he will attribute similar phenomena to a general cause; rarely will he think of the immediate cause.

*

No intelligent man experiences a minor stupidity.

*

In every work of art, great or small, and down to the smallest detail, everything depends on the initial conception.

*

There is no such thing as poetry without tropes as poetry is a single trope writ large.

15

*

A kindly old examiner whispers into a schoolboy's ear: '*Etiam nihil didicisti*' [you haven't learnt anything as yet] and gives him a pass-mark.

*

Excellence is unfathomable; tackle it in what way you will.

*

Aemilium Paulum – virum in tantum landandum, in quantum intelligi virtus potest. [Aemilius Paulus – a man to be praised as highly as virtue can be understood.]

*

I was intent on pursuing what is general until such time as I came to comprehend the achievement of outstanding people in what is particular.

*

You really only know when you know little; doubt grows with knowledge.

*

It's really a person's mistakes that make him endearing.

*

Bonus vir semper tiro. [A good man is always a beginner.]

*

There are people who love and seek out those like themselves, and, then again, those who love and pursue their opposites.

*

Anyone who had always allowed himself to take so poor a view of the world as our adversaries make out would have turned into a rotten subject.

*

Envy and hatred limit the observer's view to the surface even if this is also associated with acumen; if this, however, goes hand in hand with kindliness and love, the observer can see right through the world and mankind; indeed, he can hope to reach the Allhighest.

*

An English critic credits me with 'panoramic ability', for which I must tender my most cordial thanks.

*

A certain measure of poetical talent is desirable for every German as the right way to cloak his condition, of whatever kind it may be, with a certain degree of worth and charm.

*

The subject-matter is visible to everyone, content is only discovered by him who has something to contribute, and form is a mystery to most.

*

People's inclinations favour what is vitally alive. And youth again forms itself by youth.

*

We may get to know the world however we choose, it will always keep a day and a night aspect.

*

Error is continually repeated in action, and that is why we must not tire of repeating in words what is true.

*

Just as in Rome, besides the Romans, there was also a people of statues, so, too, apart from this real world, there is also an illusory world, mightier almost, where the majority live.

*

People are like the Red Sea: the staff has hardly kept them apart, immediately afterwards they flow together again.

*

The historian's duty: to distinguish truth from falsehood, certainty from uncertainty, doubtful matters from those which are to be rejected.

*

Only someone to whom the present is important writes a chronicle.

*

Thoughts recur, convictions perpetuate themselves; circumstances pass by irretrievably.

*

Among all peoples, the Greeks have dreamt life's dream most beautifully.

*

Translators are to be regarded as busy matchmakers who exalt the great loveliness of a half-veiled beauty: they kindle an irresistible longing for the original.

*

We like to rate Antiquity higher than ourselves, but not posterity. It's only a father who doesn't envy a son's talent.

*

It's not at all hard to subordinate yourself; but when you are set on a declining course, in the descendant, how hard it is to admit that what is, in fact, below you is above you!

21

*

Our whole achievement is to give up our existence in order to exist.

*

All we devise and do is exhausting; happy the man who doesn't get weary.

*

'Hope is the second soul of those who are unfortunate.'

*

'*L'amour est un vrai recommenceur.*' [Love is truly a new beginning.]

*

There is, too, in man a desire to serve; hence French chivalry is a form of service, '*servage*'.

*

'In the theatre visual and aural entertainment greatly limit reflection.'

*

Experience can be extended into infinity; in not quite the same sense theory can be purified and perfected. To the former the universe is open in all directions; the latter remains locked within the confines of human capacity. This is why all modes of conceptual thinking are bound to reappear, and that is why, strangely enough, a theory of limited value can regain favour in spite of wider experience.

*

It is always the same world which lies open to our view, is always contemplated or surmised, and it is always the same people who live in truth or wrong-headedly, more comfortably in the latter way than in the former.

*

Truth is contrary to our nature, not so error, and this for a very simple reason: truth demands that we should recognize ourselves as limited, error flatters us that, in one way or another, we are unlimited.

*

It is now nearly twenty years since all Germans 'transcend'. Once they notice this, they are bound to realize how odd they are.

*

It is natural enough that people should imagine they can still do what they were once able to do; that others imagine themselves capable of doing what they never could do is perhaps strange but not infrequent.

*

At all times only individuals have had an effect on scientific knowledge, not the epoch. It was the epoch that did Socrates to death by poison, the epoch that burnt Huss: epochs have always remained true to type.

*

This is true symbolism, where the particular represents the general, not as dream and shadow, but as a live and immediate revelation of the unfathomable.

*

As soon as the ideal makes a demand on the real, it in the end consumes it and also itself. Thus credit (paper money) consumes silver and its own self.

*

Mastery is often seen as egoism.

*

As soon as good works and their merit cease, sentimentality immediately takes over in the case of Protestants.

*

If you can seek out good advice, it's as though you yourself have the capacity for action.

*

There's nothing clever that hasn't been thought of before – you've just got to try to think it all over again.

*

How can we learn self-knowledge? Never by taking thought but rather by action. Try to do your duty and you'll soon discover what you're like.

*

But what is your duty? The demands of the day.

*

The reasonable world is to be seen as a great individual not subject to mortality and forever bringing about what is needed, in this way even mastering chance events.

*

The longer I live, the more depressing I find the spectacle of a man, whose optimal function is to be a lord over nature so as to free himself and his fellow men from tyrannical necessity, doing the exact opposite of what he really wants to do, and all because of some preconceived false notion; and in the end, because the structure of the project as a whole has been ruined, he just muddles on miserably with odd details.

*

Man of ability and action, be worthy of, and expect:

grace	–from those who are great
favour	–from the powerful
a helping hand	–from those who are active and good
affection	–from the crowd
love	–from an individual

*

When a dilettante has done what lies within his capacity to complete a work, he usually makes the excuse that of course it's as yet unfinished. Clearly, it never can be finished because it was never properly started. The master of his art, by means of a few strokes, produces a finished work; fully worked out or not, it is already completed. The cleverest kind of dilettante gropes about in uncertainties and, as the work proceeds, the dubiousness of the initial structure becomes more and more apparent. Right at the end the faulty nature of the work, impossible to correct, shows up clearly and so, of course, the work can never be finished.

*

For true art there is no such thing as preparatory schooling, but there are certainly preparations; the best, however, is when the least pupil takes a share in the master's work. Colour-grinders have turned into very good artists.

*

Copycat work, casually stimulating people's natural activity in imitating an important artist who achieves with ease what is difficult, is quite a different matter.

*

We are quite convinced that it is essential for the artist to make studies from nature; we won't however deny that it often grieves us to perceive the misuse of such praiseworthy endeavours.

*

We are convinced that the young artist should rarely, if at all, set out to do studies from nature without at the same time considering how he might round off every sheet and make a whole of it, transforming this unit into a pleasing picture set within a frame, and offer it courteously to the amateur and the expert.

*

Much that is beautiful stands as an isolated entity in the world, but the spirit has to discover connections and thus to create works of art. The flower unfolds its full beauty only through the insect that clings to it, through the dewdrop that makes it glisten, through the calix from out of which it may be drawing its last sustenance. No bush, no tree whose charm may not be enhanced by a neighbouring rock or brook, by a simple prospect in the distance. And so it is with human figures and so with animals of every kind.

*

The advantages accruing to a young artist in this way are indeed manifold. He learns to think out the best way of fitting together related things and, when he thus composes intelligently, he will, in the end, assuredly not lack what is termed invention, the capacity to develop a manifold whole out of single units.

*

And, as well as conforming to the tenets of art pedagogy, he gains the great advantage, by no means to be despised, of learning to create saleable pictures that are a pleasure and delight to the art lover.

*

A work of this kind need not be complete down to the last detail; if it is well envisaged, thought out and finished, it is often more appealing to the art lover than a larger, more fully completed picture.

*

Let every young artist take a look at the studies in his sketch book and portfolio and consider how many of these sheets he might have been able to make enjoyable and desirable in this way.

*

We are not talking about the higher regions of art which might of course also be discussed; this is no more than a warning to recall the artist from a devious path and point the way to higher regions.

31

*

Let the artist put this to a practical test, if only for half a year, and not make use of either charcoal or brush unless he has the firm intention of actually structuring a picture out of the natural object or scene confronting him. If he has inborn talent, what we intended by our comments will soon be revealed.

*

Tell me with whom you consort and I will tell you who you are; if I know how you spend your time, then I know what might become of you.

*

Every individual must think in his own personal way; for on his way he always finds a truth or a kind of truth which helps him get through life. But he mustn't let himself go, he has got to keep a check on himself; purely naked instinct is unseemly.

*

Absolute activity, of whatever kind, ultimately leads to bankruptcy.

*

In the works of man as in those of nature, what most deserves notice is his intention.

*

People are at a loss with regard to themselves and one another because they use means as ends, and then, because of sheer busyness, nothing whatever happens or perhaps, even worse, something which is disagreeable.

*

What we think out, what we undertake, should have achieved such perfect clarity and beauty that anything the world could do to it could only spoil it; this would leave us with the advantage of only having to adjust what has been misplaced and refashion what has been destroyed.

*

Whole, half- and quarter-errors are most difficult and wearisome to put right, to sort out.

*

Truth need not always take corporeal form; enough for it to be around in spiritual form, bringing about harmony as it floats on the breeze as a spiritual presence like the solemn-friendly sound of bells.

*

When I ask young German artists, even those who have spent some time in Italy, why they use such crudely bright colours, especially in their landscapes, and seem to shun anything like harmony, they are apt to answer boldly and cheerfully that this is precisely how they see nature.

*

Kant has drawn our attention to the fact that there is such a thing as a Critique of Reason, and that this, the highest faculty possessed by man, has cause to keep watch over itself. Let everyone judge for himself what great advantages the voice of Kant has brought him. I, for my part, would similarly like to urge that a Critique of the Senses should be worked out, if art, especially German art, is in any way to recover and to proceed and progress at a pleasing and lively pace.

*

Man, born to be a creature of reason, nevertheless needs much education, whether this comes gradually by way of careful parents and tutors, by peaceful example or by stern experience. Similarly, there is such a thing as a born potential artist, but no one is born perfect. He may have an inborn clarity of vision, a happy eye for shape, proportion, movement: but without becoming aware of this lack, he may be without a natural instinct for composition in its higher aspects, for correct tonal proportion, for light, shade and colouring.

*

Now if he is not inclined to learn from more highly skilled contemporary or earlier artists what he himself lacks in order to be a true artist, he will lag behind his own potential because of a wrong-headed idea that he is safeguarding his own originality; for we own not just what we are born with, but also what we can acquire, and this is what we are.

*

General notions and great conceit are always potential creators of shocking misfortune.

*

'You don't play the flute just by blowing – you've got to move your fingers.'

*

Botanists have a plant-category which they call 'Incompletae'; similarly one can say that there are incomplete and uncompleted people. These are the ones whose longings and strivings are out of proportion with what they actually do and what they achieve.

*

The least gifted man can be complete if he keeps within the limits of his capacities and skills, but real excellence is obscured, cancelled out and destroyed if there is not that absolutely essential sense of proportion. This disastrous lack is bound to crop up frequently in our own day; for who can possibly keep up with the demands of an exorbitant present, and that at maximum speed?

*

Only those people who are both clever and active, who are clear about their own capacities and can use them with moderation and common sense, will really get on in the world as it is.

*

A great failing: to see yourself as more than you are and to value yourself at less than your true worth.

*

From time to time I meet a young man whom I wouldn't wish different or improved in any way; but what worries me is that some of these people seem to me just the kind who let themselves drift along with the current of the stream of time, and this is where I keep wanting to point out that man is put at the helm of his own fragile craft precisely so that he may not follow the whim of the waves, the determination of his own insight.

*

But how is a young man independently to reach the insight that what everyone else pursues, approves and furthers may be reprehensible and damaging? Why shouldn't he let himself and his own natural disposition go the same way?

*

The greatest evil of our time – which lets nothing come to fruition – is, I think, that one moment consumes the next, wastes the day within that same day and so is always living from hand to mouth without achieving anything of substance. Don't we already have news-sheets for every point of the day! A clever man might well be able to slip in one or two more. In this way everything that anyone does, is working at or writing, indeed plans to write, is dragged out into the open. No one is allowed to be happy or miserable except as a pastime for the rest of the world, and so news rushes from house to house, from town to town, from one country to another, and, in the end, from one continent to the next, and all on the principle of speed and velocity.

*

As little as steam engines can be quelled, so little is this possible in the behavioural realm: the lively pace of trade, the rapid rush of paper-money, the inflated increase of debts made in order to pay off other debts, these are the monstrous elements to which a young man is now exposed. How good for him if nature has

39

endowed him with a moderate and calm attitude so that he makes no disproportionate claims on the world nor yet allows it to determine his course!

*

But the spirit of the day threatens him in every sphere and nothing is more important than to make him realize early enough the direction in which his will should steer.

*

As one grows older, the most innocent talk and action grow in significance, and to those I see around me for any length of time I always try to point out the shades of difference between sincerity, frankness and indiscretion, and that there is really no difference between them, but just an intangible transition from the most harmless comment to the most damaging, and that this subtle transition has to be observed or indeed felt.

*

In this matter we have to use tact, else we run the risk of losing people's favour without being in the least aware of this and precisely in the way we came by it. This we probably come to understand in the course of life, but only after we have paid a high price for our experience, and from this we cannot, alas, spare those who come after us.

*

The relationship of the arts and the sciences to life is very varied according to the way their temporal stages are related to the nature of their epoch and a thousand other chance contingencies; which is why it isn't easy to make sense of all this.

Poetry is most effective at the start of any set of circumstances, irrespective of whether these are quite crude, half-cultured, or when a culture is in the process of change as it begins to become aware of a foreign culture; in such cases one can claim the effect of the new is definitely to be felt.

*

Music at its best hardly needs to be new; indeed, the older it is, the more familiar to us, the more effective it can be.

*

The dignity of art perhaps appears most eminent in music because it has no material of a kind for which detailed accounting might be needed. It is all form and content and it heightens and ennobles all it expresses.

*

Music is either sacred or profane. What is sacred accords completely with its nobility, and this is where music most immediately influences life; such influence remains unchanged at all times and in every epoch. Profane music should be altogether cheerful.

*

Music of a kind that mixes the sacred with the profane is godless and shoddy music which goes in for expressing feeble, wretched, deplorable feelings, and is just insipid. For it is not serious enough to be sacred and it lacks the chief quality of the opposite kind: cheerfulness.

*

The numinous nature of church music, the cheerfulness and playfulness of folk melodies are the two pivots of true music. At these two focal points music always and inevitably leads either towards reverence or else to dance. Any mixture of the two is confusing, dilution is boring, and if music consorts with didactic or descriptive poems and texts of that kind, the result is coldness.

*

Plastic art is really only effective at its highest level; it is true that the middle zone can perhaps impress us for more reasons than one, but all middle-range art of this kind is more confusing than gladdening.

43

Sculpture therefore has to discover subject-matter of interest and this is to be found in the portraits of people of some significance. But here, too, it has to reach a high degree of excellence if it is to be at the same time true and dignified.

*

Painting is the slackest and most easy-going of all the arts. The slackest because, on account of the material and subject-matter, we condone and enjoy much that is no more than skilled craftsmanship and can hardly be called art. In part it is also because a good technical performance, even though it may be dull, can be admired by the cultured as well as the uneducated, and need only remotely resemble art in order to be highly acceptable. True colours, surfaces and a true relationship of visible objects – all this is in itself pleasing; and, since the eye is in any case used to seeing everything, it does not find misshapen or mistaken form as objectionable as a jarring note is for the listening ear. We tolerate the worst portrayal because we are used to seeing even worse originals. So the painter need only be remotely artistic so as to find a bigger public than a musician of equal merit; the minor painter can at least always operate on his own, whereas the minor musician has to associate with others in order to achieve some sort of resonance by means of a combined musical effort.

*

The question 'Are we to compare or not to compare when considering works of art' is one we would like to answer as follows: the trained connoisseur should make comparisons, for he has a general idea, a pre-conceived notion of what could be and should be achieved; the amateur, still involved in the process of being educated, can make the best progress if he does not compare but judges each achievement on its individual merit: this gradually forms an instinct and idea for the general situation. Comparison by the unknowing is really only a lazy and conceited way of avoiding judgement.

*

To find and to appreciate goodness everywhere is the sign of a love of truth.

*

The sign of a historical feeling for humanity is that, at the same time as we appreciate the merits and attainments of the present, we also take into account the merits of the past.

*

The best we get from history is that it rouses our enthusiasm.

*

Idiosyncrasy calls forth idiosyncrasy.

*

One has to remember that there are quite a lot of people who would like to say something significant without being productive, and then the most peculiar things see the light of day.

*

People who think deeply and seriously are on bad terms with the public.

*

If I'm to listen to someone else's opinion, it must be put in a positive way; I have enough problematic speculations in my own head.

*

Superstition is innate in the human make-up, and when you think you have completely ousted it, it takes refuge in the strangest nooks and crannies and then suddenly emerges when one thinks one is tolerably safe.

*

47

We would know much more about things if we weren't intent on discerning them too precisely. For, surely, an object can only be comprehensible to us when viewed at an angle of forty-five degrees.

*

Microscopes and telescopes really only serve to confuse the unaided human senses.

*

I hold my peace about many things; for I don't like to confuse people and am quite content if they are happy while I am cross.

*

Everything that liberates our mind without at the same time imparting self-control is pernicious.

*

The 'what' of a work of art interests people more than the 'how'; they can grasp the subject-matter in detail but not the method as a whole. That is why they pick out individual passages, in which, if you observe closely, the total effect is not actually lost but remains unconscious to all.

*

And the question, too, 'Where has the poet got it from?' gets no further than the 'what'; it helps no one to understand the 'how'.

*

Imagination is only ordered and structured by poetry. There is nothing more awful than imagination devoid of taste.

*

Mannerism is an ideology gone wrong, a subjective ideology; that's why, as a rule, it isn't without wit.

49

*

The philologist is dependent on the congruence of what has been handed down in written form. There is a basic manuscript and this has real gaps, errors of transcription which lead to a break in the meaning and to other difficulties common to manuscript tradition. Then a second copy is found, a third one; collating these leads to growing perception of what makes sense and meaning in the transmitted material. Indeed, the philologist goes further and requires that it should increasingly reveal and structure its inner meaning and the congruence of its subject-matter without dependence on philological aides. This calls for a special degree of sensitive judgement, a special absorption in an author long dead and a certain amount of inventive power; one cannot, therefore, take it amiss if the philologist allows himself to make a judgement in matters of taste even if this doesn't always succeed.

*

The poet is dependent on representation, the climax of which is reached when it vies with reality, that is, when the descriptions are so full of living power that everyone can see them as being actually present. At the summit of its excellence poetry appears as something completely external; the more it withdraws into the inner realm, the more it is on its way towards sinking. The kind of poetry which concentrates on the inner realm without giving it outward substance or without allowing the outward to be perceived through the inward – both are the last steps from which poetry steps down into ordinary life.

*

Oratory is dependent on all the advantages of poetry, on all its rights. It takes possession of these and misuses them in order to get hold of certain outer momentary advantages, whether moral or immoral, in civic life.

*

Literature is the fragment of fragments; only the least amount of what has happened and has been spoken was written down, the least of what has been recorded in writing has survived.

*

Although Lord Byron's talent is wild and uncomfortable in its structure, hardly anyone can compare with him in natural truth and grandeur.

*

The really important value of folksong, so called, is that its themes are taken directly from nature. But the educated poet too might well avail himself of this advantage if only he knew how to set about it.

*

But the advantage inherent in folksong is that natural people, as distinct from the educated, are on better terms with what is laconic.

*

Shakespeare is dangerous reading for talents in the process of formation: he forces them to reproduce him, and they imagine they are producing themselves.

*

Nobody can make judgements about history except those who have experienced history as a part of their own development. This applies to whole nations. The Germans have only been able to judge literature since the point they themselves have had literature.

*

One is really only alive when one enjoys the good will of others.

*

Piety is not an end but a means to attain by the greatest peace of mind the highest degree of culture.

*

This is why we may say that those who parade piety as a purpose and an aim mostly turn into hypocrites.

*

'When one is old one has to do more than when one was young.'

*

A duty absolved still feels like an unpaid debt, because one can never quite live up to one's expectations.

*

Human failings are only descried by an unloving person; that is why, in order to realize them, one has to become unloving oneself, but not more than is strictly to the purpose.

*

It is our greatest good fortune to have our failings corrected and our faults adjusted.

*

Three things are not recognized except in the due course of time:
>a hero in wartime,
>a wise man in a rage,
>a friend in need.

*

Three classes of fools:
>men because of pride,
>girls by love,
>women by jealousy.

*

The following are mad:
>he who tries to teach simpletons,
>contradicts the wise,
>is moved by empty speeches,
>believes whores,
>entrusts secrets to the garrulous.

*

Man can only live together with his own kind and not with them either; for in the long run he cannot bear the thought that anyone is like him.

*

The most mediocre novel is still better than mediocre readers, indeed the worst novel still participates in some way in the excellence of the genre as a whole.

*

Actors win hearts and don't give away their own; they cheat, but do it with charm.

*

The Germans know how to correct, but not how to give supportive help.

*

Whichever way you look at nature, it is the source of what is infinite.

*

You have to have actually found a thing if you want to know where it is situated.

*

He who acts as though he's glad, and is glad about what he has done, is happy.

1. BOCCACCIO · *Mrs Rosie and the Priest*
2. GERARD MANLEY HOPKINS · *As kingfishers catch fire*
3. *The Saga of Gunnlaug Serpent-tongue*
4. THOMAS DE QUINCEY · *On Murder Considered as One of the Fine Arts*
5. FRIEDRICH NIETZSCHE · *Aphorisms on Love and Hate*
6. JOHN RUSKIN · *Traffic*
7. PU SONGLING · *Wailing Ghosts*
8. JONATHAN SWIFT · *A Modest Proposal*
9. *Three Tang Dynasty Poets*
10. WALT WHITMAN · *On the Beach at Night Alone*
11. KENKŌ · *A Cup of Sake Beneath the Cherry Trees*
12. BALTASAR GRACIÁN · *How to Use Your Enemies*
13. JOHN KEATS · *The Eve of St Agnes*
14. THOMAS HARDY · *Woman much missed*
15. GUY DE MAUPASSANT · *Femme Fatale*
16. MARCO POLO · *Travels in the Land of Serpents and Pearls*
17. SUETONIUS · *Caligula*
18. APOLLONIUS OF RHODES · *Jason and Medea*
19. ROBERT LOUIS STEVENSON · *Olalla*
20. KARL MARX AND FRIEDRICH ENGELS · *The Communist Manifesto*
21. PETRONIUS · *Trimalchio's Feast*
22. JOHANN PETER HEBEL · *How a Ghastly Story Was Brought to Light by a Common or Garden Butcher's Dog*
23. HANS CHRISTIAN ANDERSEN · *The Tinder Box*
24. RUDYARD KIPLING · *The Gate of the Hundred Sorrows*
25. DANTE · *Circles of Hell*
26. HENRY MAYHEW · *Of Street Piemen*
27. HAFEZ · *The nightingales are drunk*
28. GEOFFREY CHAUCER · *The Wife of Bath*
29. MICHEL DE MONTAIGNE · *How We Weep and Laugh at the Same Thing*
30. THOMAS NASHE · *The Terrors of the Night*
31. EDGAR ALLAN POE · *The Tell-Tale Heart*
32. MARY KINGSLEY · *A Hippo Banquet*
33. JANE AUSTEN · *The Beautifull Cassandra*
34. ANTON CHEKHOV · *Gooseberries*
35. SAMUEL TAYLOR COLERIDGE · *Well, they are gone, and here must I remain*
36. JOHANN WOLFGANG VON GOETHE · *Sketchy, Doubtful, Incomplete Jottings*
37. CHARLES DICKENS · *The Great Winglebury Duel*
38. HERMAN MELVILLE · *The Maldive Shark*
39. ELIZABETH GASKELL · *The Old Nurse's Story*
40. NIKOLAY LESKOV · *The Steel Flea*

41. HONORÉ DE BALZAC · *The Atheist's Mass*
42. CHARLOTTE PERKINS GILMAN · *The Yellow Wall-Paper*
43. C.P. CAVAFY · *Remember, Body . . .*
44. FYODOR DOSTOEVSKY · *The Meek One*
45. GUSTAVE FLAUBERT · *A Simple Heart*
46. NIKOLAI GOGOL · *The Nose*
47. SAMUEL PEPYS · *The Great Fire of London*
48. EDITH WHARTON · *The Reckoning*
49. HENRY JAMES · *The Figure in the Carpet*
50. WILFRED OWEN · *Anthem For Doomed Youth*
51. WOLFGANG AMADEUS MOZART · *My Dearest Father*
52. PLATO · *Socrates' Defence*
53. CHRISTINA ROSSETTI · *Goblin Market*
54. *Sindbad the Sailor*
55. SOPHOCLES · *Antigone*
56. RYŪNOSUKE AKUTAGAWA · *The Life of a Stupid Man*
57. LEO TOLSTOY · *How Much Land Does A Man Need?*
58. GIORGIO VASARI · *Leonardo da Vinci*
59. OSCAR WILDE · *Lord Arthur Savile's Crime*
60. SHEN FU · *The Old Man of the Moon*
61. AESOP · *The Dolphins, the Whales and the Gudgeon*
62. MATSUO BASHŌ · *Lips too Chilled*
63. EMILY BRONTË · *The Night is Darkening Round Me*
64. JOSEPH CONRAD · *To-morrow*
65. RICHARD HAKLUYT · *The Voyage of Sir Francis Drake Around the Whole Globe*
66. KATE CHOPIN · *A Pair of Silk Stockings*
67. CHARLES DARWIN · *It was snowing butterflies*
68. BROTHERS GRIMM · *The Robber Bridegroom*
69. CATULLUS · *I Hate and I Love*
70. HOMER · *Circe and the Cyclops*
71. D. H. LAWRENCE · *Il Duro*
72. KATHERINE MANSFIELD · *Miss Brill*
73. OVID · *The Fall of Icarus*
74. SAPPHO · *Come Close*
75. IVAN TURGENEV · *Kasyan from the Beautiful Lands*
76. VIRGIL · *O Cruel Alexis*
77. H. G. WELLS · *A Slip under the Microscope*
78. HERODOTUS · *The Madness of Cambyses*
79. *Speaking of Siva*
80. *The Dhammapada*